MIDDLE FRANCONIA
Between
ROTHENBURG and NUREMBERG

ROTHENBURG

Imprint:

Elmar Hahn Verlag, Raiffeisenstr. 2, 97209 Veitshöchheim, Germany – www.elmar-hahn-verlag.de

Idea and Concept: Elmar Hahn and Klaus Schinagl
Photography: Herbert Liedel, Nuremberg
except for pages
Elmar Hahn (page: 23 above, 29, 30, 31, 42+43, 62/63, 69, 70/71, 72/73, 79, 102/103, 122/123, 126/127, 128/129, 130/131, 140/141); Jürgen Wackenhut (page: 82/83, 107 above, 108, 109, 112, 118/119); Hans Raab (page: 92/93, 114/115, 134/135); Michel Vogel (page: 32/33, 50, 138/139); Schreyer-Löbl (page: 136/137, 139 above); Waltraud Klammet (2. Cover, page: 51); Thomas Peter Widmann (page: 18 below, 68); Luftbild Bröll (page: 90/91, 94/95); Toni Schneiders (page: 81 above and below); Guido Mehl (page: 78); Wolfgang Bouillon (page: 89); Klammet and Aberl (page: 99); Josef Stöhr (page: 110/111); Horst Glanz (page: 113); Helmut Gruber (page: 116/117); Wolfgang Grötsch (page: 132/133); Manuel Berninger (page: 142 below)

Text: Kurt Endres, Nuremberg
English interpretation: Tina Neil, Würzburg
Layout: Design by Schinagl, Veitshöchheim
Preprinting: Schinagl produktion + media, Veitshöchheim
Production: Karo Druck OHG, Frangart

ISBN 3-928645-28-5

Following pages: The hills of the Hersbrucker Schweiz Region

MIDDLE FRANCONIA

Between

nd NUREMBERG

Photography: Herbert Liedel and others
Text: Kurt Endres
English: Tina Neil
Layout: Klaus Schinagl

elmar hahn verlag

The Middle Franconian Panorama

Is it possible to describe a region like Middle Franconia in a guide book in such a way as to do it justice? Every well thought-through entry and choice of topics brings to mind the numerous sights and places of interest that had to be omitted due to a lack of space.

The geographic location and the varying geological structures mean significant differences in climate and soil quality and thus have always provided a variety of natural opportunities and challenges for the economy of the region. Swabian, Franconian, Slavic and Bavarian influences joined forces here and left their marks in dialects and customs. Free imperial cities, margraves, bishops, monasteries and abbeys as well as the local nobility all competed for power and influence.

Capable men with a sense of perception inhabited the region from early on beginning with the skilled craftsmen of modern times developing into a permanent trade fair for inventors in Nuremberg. The city which was formerly renowned for its industrial products has been undergoing a change and is in the process of making a name for itself in the high-tech sector. It has already established itself in the network of European high-tech centers. The newly-created Franconian Lakes have surpassed all expectations in their success as a tourist region.

It seems almost impossible to mention all the aspects that attract people to Middle Franconia. The photographer, Herbert Liedel, and the author, Kurt Endres, two dyed-in-the-wool Franconians, have attempted through photography and text to offer a closer glimpse of Middle Franconia. Both have worked together to help the tourist become more easily acquainted with some of the places of interest and landmarks in the region.

This book is an attempt to combine useful information and anecdotal historical facts. Both men are well-versed in their subject matter and are contributing to a long tradition derived from a deep commitment to their homeland.

Contents

The Panorama of Middle Franconia

Urban Economic Center and Rural Structures

Bavarian King Ludwig I divided Franconia in three parts in 1837. The so-called middle part is the most varied, somewhat motley in nature and loosely meshed or lumped together. The 7,246 square kilometer area has 1.6 million inhabitants putting it in third place after Upper Bavaria and Swabia in population density in the state of Bavaria.

The spread in population within the region varies immensely. The industrial city of Nuremberg is second only to Munich in its number of inhabitants (431 inhabitants per square kilometer). On the other hand, the western part of Middle Franconia has the lowest population density in Bavaria (95 inhabitants per square kilometer). A similar gap is evident when a comparison is made between the economic purchasing power and infrastructure of the two regions. In both cases, the western part of Middle Franconia is at a definite disadvantage.

Scenic Variety

The variety of characteristics that make up Middle Franconia is set forth in the variety of geological formations indigenous to the region. The western part has fertile loessial layers of soil covering the shell limestone. Moving eastwards, the keuper hills of the Steigerwald Wood and the Franconian Plateau come into view along with deciduous forests growing in sandstone, clay and marly soils and, in-between, there is a modest amount of agriculture at less high elevations. Infertile sandy soil in the Nuremberg Basin is replaced with sandstone and the clay soils of the Black Jura further east. And finally, the ferruginous sandstone and limestone walls of the Franconian Alb rise up. The highest elevation in Middle Franconia is the 650-meter high Hesselberg Hill in the southern part of the Franconian Alb.

The Nuremberg "Grit Hole of the Reich" has extensive areas of fir trees in the Lorenzer and Sebalder imperial forests, planted around 650 years ago and said to be the first artificial forests in the world. The Stromers, a patrician family from Nuremberg, had these forests planted for various economic reasons – one important one was to insure the supply of honey for the city.

As a part of the south German stratum layer landscape, Middle Franconia is of great geological interest. Rivers that once

flowed south in the direction of the Danube were corroded by the feeders of the Rhine and were forced to flow into the tributaries of the Rhine. The same thing happened to the Rednitz water system, to the Pegnitz and the Tauber rivers.

The result: a characteristic river triangle in the middle of the region including the Aisch in the northwest, the Franconian Rezat in the southwest and the Rednitz Furrow as the north-south axis in the east. Include the Pegnitz and the Altmühl as well and we have the main lines of transportation and inhabited areas.

A Mosaic of History

The history of Middle Franconia is as varied as its scenery. Varied because time and again, one family dynasty was dissolved in favor of another powerful noble family and there was a continual juggling of property claims and ownership. All of these factors played a decisive role in the region's political and economic development.

The most powerful players were the free imperial cities and their often vast territories. Then came the burgraves and margraves that concentrated their power in the countryside. Not to be forgotten were the cleric leaders who wielded their influence as prince-bishops, bishops or abbots. The best example in Middle Franconia is the Cistercian Abbey in Heilsbronn. The

Below: A view of Nuremberg in the 16th century from Schedel's "Chronicle of the World".

Knights of the Teutonic Order had their own establishment in the middle of Nuremberg including their own working quarters and jurisdiction; they even maintained actual borders to the rest of the city.

Further power players included knights and the nobility, influential families of noble descent that understood the importance of marrying into the right family and inheriting the right land in order to exert the required amount of wide-reaching power. A certain Eppelein von Gailingen or a Götz von Berlichingen made life extremely difficult for the free imperial cities.

Unlike the ignominious knights who resorted to all types of exploitations in order to secure their positions, the Seckendorff family had their own means of wielding power. The family line probably started out on a small piece of land near Cadolzburg and rose to the position of imperial estate officials. They married into several influential families that controlled a major portion of the Rangau Region, the center of the western part of Middle Franconia. Their family crest can still be seen from the environs of Cadolzburg all the way to Windsheim and their double red and blue castle in Oberzenn is an appropriate reminder of their importance.

Changing Times

After the fall of the Berlin Wall and the reopening of the borders to eastern Europe, Middle Franconia reestablished the central position that Nuremberg had enjoyed as the crossroads of major trade routes in the Middle Ages. Both the city of Nuremberg and the region itself have accepted this new challenge. Nuremberg's importance as an international convention center has multiplied and high-tech and logistics companies have mushroomed. In the meantime, the western part of Middle Franconia has been linked to the highway network and supra-regional shopping malls. Continued development of the Franconian Plateau of Lakes is a must.

Above: Arduous work: separating the hops while taking time for a chat.
Right: 16th century view of bear-hunting in front of the gates of Lauf.

Milestones in History

81-96	Roman palisade wall built under Emperor Domitian; Castellum Biricianis (Weißenburg) erected
258	Franks first appear in history as an amalgamation of several Germanic tribes
482-511	Franks become Christians under Clodwig; beginning of the Middle Ages
793	Fossa Carolina near Treuchtlingen: a canal begun by Charlemagne to connect the Main and the Danube rivers
919	Eastern Frankish empire becomes the "German empire"
1050	"nuorinberch" mentioned in the Sigena Certificate; Nuremberg founded under Salian Emperor Heinrich III
1116-1196	Hohenstaufen dynasty attempts to establish a hereditary duchy in "Rothenburg"
1138-1152	Reign of Konrad III, his sons are the dukes of Rothenburg
1152-1190	Construction of imperial palace in Nuremberg under Frederick I Barbarossa
1216	Ellingen becomes a seat of the Teutonic Order
1256-1273	Great Interregnum during which the crown is contested between Richard of Cornwall and Alfonso X
1273-1291	Flourishing of the cities, especially the free imperial cities, begins under Rudolf I (Hapsburg)
1261-1297	In his capacity as burgrave of Nuremberg, Frederick III increases the size of the county

1314-1347	Nuremberg flourishes under Ludwig the Bavarian; charitable hospitals are established
1331	The office of the bailiff of Ansbach is turned over to the burgraves of Nuremberg
1348-1352	Pogrom and plague in Germany and Europe
1356	Golden Bull (Karl IV): every newly-elected king holds his first Imperial Diet in Nuremberg
1363	Burgraves of Nuremberg are made imperial princes
1376-1377	Heinrich Toppler of Rothenberg commands the troops of the free imperial cities in the First War of the Swabian League
1388	The Princes Army defeats the Army of the Swabian League whose power is then broken
1415-1417	Mark Brandenburg and the title of imperial elector are both granted to burgrave Frederick VI of Nuremberg; burgraves become margraves
1424	Transfer of imperial crown jewels to Nuremberg
1440-1486	Albrecht Achilles, margrave of Ansbach, becomes elector of Brandenburg in 1470
1449-1453	First Margrave War
1471-1528	Albrecht Dürer, universal genius from Nuremberg
1495	Imperial Knights of the Franks organize the Knights of the Frankish Circle
1503-1505	War of the Landshuter Succession: Nuremberg increases its territory considerably
1524-1525	Peasants' War and defeat of the Peasants' Army by Margrave Kasimir
1525	Nuremberg introduces the Reformation; other cities and the principality of Ansbach under margrave George the Pious follow suit
1541-1557	Albrecht Alkibiades, margrave of Kulmbach begins the Second Margrave War
1618-1648	Thirty Years' War
1631	Rothenberg is captured by the head of the Bavarian Army, Tilly
1632	Gustav Adolf confronts the Imperial Army at the Alte Veste or Old Fortress near Zirndorf
1637-1657	Members of Upper Austrian religious sects immigrate to Middle Franconia under Ferdinand III
after 1685	Early industrialization introduced after the Huguenots settle in Erlangen and Schwabach
1743	University in Erlangen is established by margrave Frederick of Bayreuth
1769	Principality of Bayreuth goes to Ansbach
1792	Margrave Alexander relinquishes his power and the principality of Ansbach-Bayreuth goes to Prussia
1803	Empire (Reichsdeputationshauptschluss) secularizes the religious principalities and suppresses the independence of the free imperial cities

Above: The old university in Altdorf attracted students from near and far including the later commander of the Austrian Army, Wallenstein, who spent a few weeks studying here.

1805-1810	Frankish Circle is dissolved, the greater portion of Franconia goes to Bavaria; western part of Rothenburger Land goes to Württemberg, building land in the Tauber valley goes to Baden
1808	Pegnitz district (capital: Nuremberg) and Rezat district (Ansbach) are created
1810	Pegnitz district terminated, Ansbach becomes the capital
1835	First German train goes from Nuremberg to Fürth
1836-1846	Ludwig-Danube-Main Canal built
1837	Rezat district is renamed Middle Franconia
1918	Bavaria becomes a republic
1934-1945	Middle and Upper Franconia become one administrative district
1972	Bavarian district reform; some of the districts are dissolved and Middle Franconia is divided into two planning regions out of a total of 16 in Bavaria: Region 7 (industrial zoning) and Region 8 (western part of Middle Franconia)
1992	New Main-Danube Canal is completed and is navigable in its entirety.
1993	Street of Human Rights at the German Museum in Nuremberg is dedicated
2000	Nuremberg celebrates its 950th anniversary
2001	Erlangen and Herzogenaurach turn 1000 years old
2000/2002	Business tower and Documentary Center become Nuremberg's new landmarks

Nuremberg – from an Imperial City to a Modern Metropolis

The city's location along a major trade route and its inventive craftsman turned an insignificant town on the Pegnitz into the wealthiest German city of the late Middle Ages.

Nuremberg in the Course of History

The beginnings of Nuremberg date back to the time of the Salian emperors. The so-called "Sigena- Certificate", which documents the manumission of a slave, demonstrates the existence of a royal estate at Nuremberg in 1050 and thus documents the city's beginnings. The royal estate was most probably located near St. Egidien Church.

The Fortress – Symbol of Power

The royal estate had to be made secure. The rocky sandstone precipice (originally "norimberga") that ascends slightly on the east side and at its spur drops off sharply on the other three sides, was the ideal strategic position for the castle that was to be erected. The original Hohenstaufen palace (now rebuilt) still stands on the west side of the fortifications.

East of this palace is the true Kaiserburg or emperor's castle with inner and outer courtyards, the latter of which contains various outbuildings, the Deep Well and the Sinwell Castle Keep. The older part of the royal castle of the burgraves of Nuremberg begins at the triangular open space which offers the best view of the city. The Hohenzollern dynasty, the traditional enemy of the later free imperial city, resided here as of 1192.

The Himmelstor or Heaven's Gate was built into the southern curtain wall of the fort in the late 14th century in order to be able to enter the city without first going through the fortifications. Although the Castle Keep was a far superior watch tower, the "Luginsland" Tower was erected in 1377. The name of the tower in German translates roughly into "look into the land or countryside" and the townspeople actually had still another nickname for the tower, "LugindieBurg" or "look into the fortress", since the main function of the tower was to keep an eye on the activities of the burgraves.

Previous pages: Nuremberg's premier landmark: the Kaiserburg including the prominent Sinwell Tower are both firmly situated on a rocky sandstone precipice.
Left: Fairytale setting with the Heidenturm or Heathen's Tower in the outer bailey.
Above: A continuous city wall with four round watchtowers protected the old town in medieval times; the Neutorturm or New Gate Tower is southwest of the Kaiserburg.

The Heidenturm or Heathen's Tower houses the two-story chapel. The imperial gallery within the chapel is characteristic of the type of architecture that was common when Nuremberg was an imperial city. Another such example can be seen in the Frauenkirche or Our Lady's Church on the north side of the Market Square that holds an outdoor Christmas market each year during the month of December. The Sebalduskirche or St. Sebald's Parish Church, the setting for festive concerts, also has such a gallery in the west choir.

The city built a large Kornhaus or Granary in the eastern part of the fortifications. Today this building houses the Youth Hostel. This structure squeezed into the summit of these rocky precipice walls contributes greatly to the overall impression of the fortifications alongside other similar patrician edifices nestled against the rocky walls below. All together, they form a unique crown for the city.

Safe Inside the Old Town Walls

Construction of the city walls began early and was completed by 1400. Improvements were continued until the Thirty Years' War and these walls provided the military protection necessary for the castle. The rugged sandstone wall interspersed with the round towers of bossed sandstone blocks is most impressive. It is five kilometers in length and encompasses the entire Old Town.

Another architectural gem of this city is the steep shingled roofs (53° slant) found in the northern Sebald Quarter of the Old Town. Even the newer buildings down to the Pegnitz River adhere to this architectural style. Bombs dropped during the Second World War destroyed almost all the medieval buildings east of the Bergstrasse.

Thick watchtowers mark the corners of the city wall. Originally square on the inside, their rounded outer walls gave testimony to advanced fortification technology. These towers are similar in design to the Sinwell Castle Keep, which was also the model for the castle towers in Lichtenau near Ansbach.

The layout of the Old Town, particularly in the northern sector, is characterized by winding narrow streets and blind alleys. On the other hand, the streets in the Lorenz Quarter are laid out in a strict east-west pattern, which simplifies getting around. The early building phases, especially the contour of the second city wall, are nevertheless still easily identifiable. Sections of the wall are evident underground.

Left: View of the 12th century double chapel's lower floor in the Heathen's Tower.
Above: Albrecht Dürer had a splendid view of the Castle and the Tiergärtnertor Square from his home (right).
Following pages: The Weißgerbergasse or Tanner's Street still resembles Nuremberg's Old Town before its destruction in WWII.

DUKE

1918

Cultural life centers around the Tiergärtnertor Square on warm summer nights and it is easy to understand why. Located at the foot of the fortress and near the Albrecht Dürer House, this is where traditional pubs, paths behind the battlements and breaks in the fortification walls to the ditches lend authenticity to the medieval atmosphere. The path to the Pegnitz River leads past some magnificent patrician houses whose ground floor walls are built of sandstone. In contrast, the buildings in the Weißgerbergasse or Tanner's Street are half-timbered, indicative of the craftsmen who lived and worked there.

Life in the Imperial City

An ongoing dualism persisted between the oligarch of the patricians and their

privileges on the one hand and the strictly-regimented guilds of the various craftsmen on the other. Even though others imperial cities in Middle Franconia slowly but surely managed to permit some type of co-determination in the city councils in the 15th and 16th centuries, Nuremberg was never successful in doing such. Even the artist Albrecht Dürer was not permitted to enter the council hall that he himself had painted when

certain prestigious families were holding balls there.

Daily life was much more difficult and complicated for the inhabitants of this imperial city than for those simple folk who lived under the rule of the despised local nobility outside the city walls. There was continual bickering between the city council and the burgraves who couldn't be forced out of the city until 1427 when their castle burned down. They resettled against their will at the Cadolzburg Fortress.

Every now and then, the emperor voiced his claims on the city. A good example is

Left: The Tiergärtnertor Square is a popular meeting spot for young people on mild summer nights.
Above: The Tugendbrunnen or Fountain of Virtues on Lorenz Square depicts various allegorical forms of human behavior.

the Market Square as it stands today. This square was the Jewish Quarter until 1349 when a pogrom left at least 542 Jews dead and the remainder of the Jewish community was expelled to the town of Fürth. Our Lady's Church was built on the site of the former synagogue.

The jewel of the Market Square is the Schöner Brunnen or Beautiful Fountain. Another treat is the daily glockenspiel, the "Männleinlauf" or "strutting men" at Our Lady's Church at twelve noon sharp. The marching men are reminiscent of the Golden Bull of 1356 in which Emperor Karl IV decreed that every newly-elected emperor had to spend the first day of his Imperial Diet in Nuremberg. The glockenspiel at the Frauenkirche shows the seven electors strutting past the emperor's throne in honor of his presence.

Charitable Foundations Play an Important Role

As the cities grew in size and wealth, the obligations of their citizens grew as well. The old, the sick and the poor had to be taken care of. Charitable foundations

built in the past still stand today and are a prominent part of the skyline. Whereas in Rothenburg, these foundations were located in a separate section of the city and surrounded by a wall and a bastion, in Nuremberg, affluent burghers donated generously to have several famous buildings erected throughout the city, buildings that are typical of the Nuremberg style and proof of the charitableness and wealth of its inhabitants.

The Sieben Zeilen or Seven Rows erected prior to 1500 for the Swabian cotton weavers south of Weaver's Square is considered to be the forerunner of the alms houses built by the Fuggers of Augsburg, the great financiers and merchants of the 15th to 19th centuries. Almost totally destroyed during the last war, they have been rebuild

Above: The half-timbered Weinstadel, the Water Tower and Hangman's Footbridge form a picturesque ensemble on the Pegnitz River.
Following pages: The 19-meter high Schöner Brunnen or Beautiful Fountain is located on the Main Market Square in front of Our Lady's Church (Frauenkirche). This 14th century fountain earns its name from the 40 ornately decorated sculptures that adorn it.

to resemble the original structures. A picture-perfect example is the buildings around the Sondersiechenkobel, a former charitable home for the infirm, which was later a wine pub or Weinstadel and has now been converted to a student dining hall – nearly a return to its original function.

Not to be forgotten is the Heilig-Geist-Spital or Holy Ghost Charitable Foundation with its double-arch across an arm of the Pegnitz. Konrad Groß donated this foundation in 1332; Hans Behaim the Elder renovated it almost completely between 1506 and 1511.This foundation is truly one of the city's landmarks and the appropriate backdrop for events such as a performance of fishermen fighting on the river known as "Pegnitz Burns".

The Patron Saints of Nuremberg

The Pegnitz divides the city and it was Emperor Ludwig the Bavarian in the mid 14th century who issued the decree that the two quarters of the city joined by their bridges had to bear the signs of the city's patron saints. Nuremberg's two main churches are named after two of the city's patron saints and one is located in each of the quarters: St. Sebald's in the northern quarter "urbs" and St. Lorenz's in the southern quarter "civitas".

The only member of the Wittelsbach family who became emperor made sure that the relics of a certain abbot Deocarus from a monastery in Herrieden on the Altmühl River found their home in Nuremberg. Deocarus was nothing less than the father confessor of Charlemagne and an altar in St. Lorenz's bearing his name is the sole reminder of Nuremberg's third patron saint. The silver shrine holding his relics was melted down after a mediation in 1806.

Rothenburg, in comparison, had and has an altar containing the "holy blood" of Christ in St. Jacob's Church and pilgrimages were made from far and wide to see the relic. These visiting pilgrims played an important economic role in this imperial city, a role that can be compared to the role of the pilgrims to Jerusalem.

Above: It's not often enough that the Christmas Market is so appropriately decked in snow.
Right: The west facade of St. Lorenz Church with its rose window is a true masterpiece of the high Gothic.

Superb Craftsmen

The main churches of Nuremberg house some world-famous treasures that made the city renowned for its creativity and works of art in the late Middle Ages. The early 16th century in Nuremberg was not only characterized by its transformation to the Reformation but by its creative productivity and willingness to donate works of art for the common good. The list of donors is the Who's Who of Nuremberg's most influential patrician families.

The "Englischer Gruß" or "English Greeting" medallion that dominates the east choir of St. Lorenz's is one of these masterpieces. It is the work of Veit Stoß and its donor was Anton Tucher in 1518. Veit Stoß was a woodcarver who throughout his life sold his carvings to the city. In 1477 he gave up his rights as a citizen and worked in Krakow and did not return to Nuremberg until 1496.

The tabernacle by the stone-carver Adam Kraft is also housed in St. Lorenz's. Kraft's figures are so perfect that it is hard to believe that they are actually out of stone. The slender tabernacle soars upwards and its delicateness makes it seem almost weightless. It was created between 1493 and 1500 and paid for by Hans Imhoff. Work on the tabernacle was interrupted several times and Imhoff did not live to see its completion although Kraft did get paid in full.

Paying for St. Sebald's tomb in St. Lorenz's was a different story. The plans for the three-tiered memorial were from

Left: The "English Greeting" medallion by Veit Stoß below the cross rib vaulting in St. Lorenz's. Below: Adam Kraft has portrayed himself at the foot of his late Gothic Tabernacle in St. Lorenz's. Following pages: The Kaiserburg and St. Sebald's in the setting sun.

an unknown artist and poured in brass by Peter Vischer in 1507. The donors were a committee of wealthy patricians consisting of Anton Tucher, Lazarus Holzschuher, Sebald Schreyer, Peter Imhoff the Elder and Sigmund Fürer. The committee did manage to donate the lion's share for the eight tons of brass, but the outstanding sum was left up to the church-goers, who were movingly encouraged to give as much as they could possibly spare.

The rear building of the Fembohaus contains the renowned Hirsvogel Hall recently restored to its former old-Nuremberg Renaissance glory. The architect in 1534 was Peter Flötner.

The fragments that could be rescued from the bombing during WWII are now on display in Tucher Castle.

Hidden Nooks and Crannies

Nuremberg with its population of a half million inhabitants offers its international tourists more than just the usual medieval sights. Take a walk down any narrow side street in the Old Town and discover nooks and crannies that have maintained their hamlet-like character: side streets northeast of the Königstrasse, the quarter north of the Ludwigstrasse and the area around St. Jacob's Market. Rooftop houses above half-timbered structures give testimony to simple trades and various crafts of bygone days.

Not to be forgotten are the mills of which more than one hundred were said to have been in use between the city walls along the Pegnitz. Only street names and squares remind the visitor today of their past importance.

Left: The reliquary of St. Sebald, one of Nuremberg's patron saints, is the work of Peter Vischer and stands in St. Sebald's.
Below: Portions of Hirsvogel Hall were brought to safety during the Second World War and the hall has been reconstructed near the Tucher Castle.

Contemporary Art

Although a stroll through the Old Town may leave the impression that time has stood still in Nuremberg, it definitely hasn't. Contemporary artists and craftsmen of world renown have received international recognition for their work here. Dealing with Nuremberg's infamous past during the Third Reich has not been easy. One reminder of this past is the row of columns next to the Germanisches Museum or German Museum. These columns inscribed with the articles of human rights in every imaginable language line the Street of Human Rights.

International acclaim has also been received for the Documentation Center housed in sections of the Convention

Hall. The city now boasts a new, taller landmark in its eastern sector as well: the business tower of a life insurance company is a modern contrast to the silhouette of the medieval fortifications.

A New Cultural Understanding

Confrontation with the past through art and documentation is only one aspect of the new approach to better cultural understanding. Alternative and contemporary art exhibits are a welcome addition to the well-known museums providing a supra-regional attraction.

The German National Museum, the Fembo House and the Toy Museum are part and parcel of the Old Town. Guided tours through Old Nuremberg are extremely popular as well. This book is meant to assist the tourist in his own exploration of the beauty and history of this city.

Nuremberg successfully combines its glorious past as an imperial city with a taste for modernity. Concerts, bardic poetry readings, jousts in the outer ditches, bicycle races around the outer walls and the Old Town Festival are just some of the events that make up Nuremberg's active cultural calender and a reason why the city attracts so many visitors each year.

Regional Significance

The entire region profits from the fact that Nuremberg is an internationally-renowned convention center and not only because it sponsors the world's largest toy fair. Specialty trade shows such as Consumenta immensely broaden the spectrum on the fairgrounds where new halls are continually being constructed to keep up with the increasing pace of foreign exhibitors.

The infrastructure and public transportation network have also been expanded and modernized to meet the challenges of a "Rock in the Park" open air festival or a home game of the local soccer club when sport fans from all over Germany flock to the new stadium to root for their team. Such events are a boon to the neighboring cities as well.

Left: The Street of Human Rights next to the German Museum was designed by the Israeli artist, Dani Karavan, and dedicated in 1993.

Castles, Ravines and Navigational Routes

Schwarzach and the Old Canal offer the ideal backdrop for stately homes and hiking in the region provides the city-dweller the peace and quiet he is looking for. This charming countryside around Nuremberg, Fürth and Schwabach is lovely no matter what the season.

The City of Fürth

The origins of Fürth ford are most probably to be found where the Stadthalle (concert hall) stands today. Near the Max Bridge, lies the ford, a medieval trade route between Frankfurt and Regensburg via the Rednitz.

The city is older than Nuremberg and was once a part of King Heinrich II's imperial possessions. It was given to the newly-founded bishopric of Bamberg at the beginning of the 11th century. The market town built around St. Michael's was continually under the authority of some local nobility and remained in the shadows of its striving neighbor, Nuremberg.

The triumvirate of the dean of the Cathedral of Bamberg, the margrave of Ansbach and the city council of the free imperial city of Nuremberg prevented Fürth from ever attaining the normal rights of a city. For a time, Fürth had Europe's second largest Jewish community after Prague. The Jewish cemetery and informative Jewish Museum bear testimony to this era.

The quarter surrounding St. Michael's still resembles a Franconian town of the 17th and 18th centuries and is a lively place with its numerous pubs and restaurants, all perfectly integrated into the medieval half-timbered buildings. This quarter has been lovingly restored and maintained and provides a romantic aura all its own.

The high point of the year is Fürth's Michaeliskirchweih, a church dedication celebration held in the middle of October. This celebration features a Harvest Parade as well as a fair with countless booths and rides for young and old alike to which thousands of visitors are attracted each year. The crowds make their way between the Town Hall and the City Theater, blind to the 17th century facades on either side of the street.

The Italianate Town Hall stands out due to its monumental size and non-German appearance. Built in 1850 in the neo-Renaissance style, it is Fürth's most famous landmark. The family tower is a loose copy of the Palazzo Vecchio in Florence and the rounded arches of the windows form a clear contrast to the Baroque and Classical buildings surrounding it.

A Risky Venture

The tolerance of the margraves towards minorities and those of different religious beliefs was a boon to the city from early on and enabled it to attract craftsmen of all trades. Mirrors and needles were two specialities that flourished in part because of the city's location on a major trade route.

Names like Grundig and Schickedanz (mail order house) are synonymous with Fürth's expansion and prosperity in the 20th century. Owners of simple workshops and general stores had the courage and vision to become global players. Everything from top quality toy manufacturers to amusement parks and soccer stadiums are associated with Fürth.

Charitable institutions and private sponsorships have helped ensure Fürth's cultural position. There are a surprising number of theaters and new museums as well as a lively pub district in the successfully-restored city center.

Previous Pages: A large portion of Thann Fortress could be kept from falling into total disrepair.
Left: The neo-Renaissance style of the Town Hall in Fürth adds a touch of Florentine ambience to the city.
Below: The City Theater in Fürth through its varied repertory attracts numerous theater-goers.

Schwabach

The arrival of the religiously persecuted Protestant Huguenots from France resulted in quite an economic upswing for the city of Schwabach. The reputation of the goldsmiths who were experts in gold leaf was soon so widespread that the city was known as the "Goldsmith City". Two of the tiny Town Hall towers were recently restored with a layer of gold leaf, an historically-accurate touch of color on the church and Town Hall Square.

Margrave Churches

It is the churches and their architecture that dot the countryside alongside a few secular buildings that remain that characterize the communities in the region.

Right: The newly-gilded roof tiles of the town hall oriel on the Königsplatz is reminiscent of Schwabach's past significance as goldsmiths.
Below: The Beautiful Fountain on the Königsplatz.

Around Schwabach and Roth, the architects commissioned by the margraves of Ansbach were responsible for the simple straight towers, void of any decoration and symbols of the Protestant faith, which can be seen throughout the region. The insides of the margrave churches often have one unusual characteristic in common: the altar, the organ and the pulpit have been placed one above the other.

Blossoming Cities

What type of influence existed outside the proud imperial free city? Who could manage to survive near these powerful economic giants? The sovereign territory of Hirschberg near Beilngries began south of the Schwarzach River, the Upper Palatinate territory of Neumarkt was to the east while the margraves from Bayreuth had their say over the Sebald Imperial Forest to the north and the margrave of Ansbach ruled in the southwest. Amongst them were also the local nobility at the Cistercian abbey in Heilsbronn and other less influential territorial nobility.

Many of these men were truly proven men of action, almost visionaries, with their far-reaching initiatives. Instead of having to adhere to the static constraints of the powerful guilds in cities such as Nuremberg, these local lords were able to invite refugees, undesired persons elsewhere, to their territories.

Jewish craftsmen and merchants, whom the guilds of Nuremberg would have nothing to do with, were more than welcome in Schnaittach. This co-existence and mutual tolerance brought advantages to everyone involved.

Luxury in the Country

Both the higher and lower nobility with their desire for and display of luxury and splendor were naturally tempted to leave the overcrowded medieval city and flee

to more comfortable stately homes in the country. The lack of a noble class in the Imperial Free City of Nuremberg was compensated for in the countryside where the patricians could imitate life at court in a far grander fashion.

The wealthy families of Nuremberg moved to the thinly-populated Imperial Forest. The moated castles of the nobility were replaced by a middle Franconian variation of a stately home next to a pond with corner towers symbolizing a defensive function. The mighty stone fortresses and castles of local princes were emulated time and again in the smaller and larger pleasure palaces with their obligatory gardens. A further reason for the move to the country was the attempt to stabilize the family fortune through agriculture and the timber trade. Water mills and hammer mills were set up and beekeepers were hired. Jobs were thus created for the locals.

Left: Tucher Castle in Simmelsdorf near Schnaittach is often referred to as Franconia's Neuschwanstein.
Above: This former patrician castle in Neunhof near Nuremberg features a Baroque garden.
Following pages: The Schwarzach Gorge near Schwarzenbruck is rather undisciplined in its romantic beauty and thus considered to be one of the most fascinating sandstone gorges in Franconia.

The Patricians from the Cities

The source of the Schwarzach River, a rather common name found in Franconia, is south of the Dillberg Massif near Neumarkt in the upper Palatinate. It makes a large bend around the massif and reaches Middle Franconia near Gnadenberg where it accompanies the Ludwig Canal for a time. On its way, it passes by a number of small hamlets before it flows into the Rednitz just north of Schwabach. A rather pleasant, unhurried river. Riders' tracks across the neighboring fields are the only signs of human incursion and the inhabitants here have learned how to let this river run its course, meandering into a wide valley instead of being straightened into a concrete corset.

This river had its heyday in the 17th and 18th centuries when the patricians from Nuremberg settled along its banks and in the adjacent countryside. The Thirty Years' War and the breaking up of the countryside into numerous small territories had robbed these rich merchants of their sinecures in commerce.

Along the Old Ludwig Canal

It is said that a person has to be from "here" to appreciate all the pine trees growing in the region. The old villages that turned woodland into arable land still thrive by serving Franconian specialities that make the mouth water at prices well below the average. This is a part of the world where festivities are part and parcel of everyday life; in other words, this is where Franconian sociability and "Gemütlichkeit" are at home.

Leave the busy city and head for the country via the Old Canal, the ideal way to escape through a corridor of green quietude.

This was not, however, the primary concern of the canal builders between 1836 and 1846. They were more interested in economic power and prestige. Following the examples of England and France, this inexpensive means of the transport of goods was to quicken the pace of economic growth in the Kingdom of Bavaria, growth that had placed it in a unique position in the German nation.

Beginning in Bamberg and cutting through the Rednitz valley upstream to Nuremberg, the Ludwig Canal climbed lock after lock until it reached the hills of the Franconian Alb before continuing on to Neumarkt, then on through the Sulz and Ottmaringer valleys to the narrow Altmühl River where it connected up with the Danube. Progress was slow in comparison with the construction of the more recent Main-Danube Canal which takes a different route but is equally important to the economy.

Hikers and cyclists alike use this canal path which is forced to cross a few insignificant regional roads. The route goes through the Lorenz Imperial Forest, a 650-year old pine forest, recorded as being the first artificial forest in the world. Cool in the summer and slippery in the winter, the tow path leads past skaters on the ice below and towns literally bursting with friendly pubs.

The infertile sandy layer of soil on top of the sandstone layer of keuper soil in the Nuremberg Basin gives way to the enriched clay soil which has been added to the sandstone of the Rhät region. The most scenic portion of the tow path begins to the east of the Pfefferhütte or Pepper Hut. The pine trees become fewer in

Above: The Old Ludwig-Danube-Main Canal crosses the Schwarzach valley via a deep sandstone bridge. At the time of its conception, its engineers were considered genuine technical pioneers.

number and a forest of deciduous trees accompanies this romantic portion of the Old Canal. Although the canal no longer serves its original function, it nevertheless provides the opportunity to see a beautiful and varied countryside.

Technical Pioneers

The Ludwig Canal reached its highest point - an elevation of 417 meters between lock 35 and 33. This was also where the canal engineers were put to the task: the canal had to cross the Rhät ravines (Distelloch Dam), it had to cut through the flanks of the hillside (Dörlbacher Cut) and supply the canal with water. Often enough, these engineers became aware of their limits as entire slopes slid out from under them or bridge substructures collapsed and the necessary water supply never materialized.

Lauf on the Pegnitz

Lauf on the Pegnitz River, however, offers a completely different cityscape. It was once important for it water mills so close to Erlangen. Today Wenceslaus Castle still bears witness to the beginnings of the Slavic influence. As a result, the Franconian dialect here is harsher and more guttural.

The city's charm is a combination of its location on the Pegnitz, its medieval walls and the Market Square dominated by the old Town Hall. Nearby is the gentle valley of dogger sandstone whose heavy sedimentation was brought about by the Pegnitz which meanders through this pleasant valley as it pleases. The high plateaus of porous limestone in the Franconian and Hersbrucker Schweiz regions to the north and east are full of deep fissures and an abundance of underground caves. This is a rock climber's paradise and a truly unique part of Middle Franconia.

Right: *Lauf – St. Leonard's and the former charitable institution.*
Below: *Wenceslaus Castle in Lauf on the Pegnitz was built around 1360 during Emperor Karl IV's reign and is known for its Wappensaal or Hall of Heraldic Crests.*

1884

Valleys Encompassed by Caves and Rocky Cliffs

Precipitous rocky cliffs and steep narrow hiking paths turn the hills on both sides of the Pegnitz River into a climber's paradise. Hikers will also enjoy exploring the numerous caves in the region and after a day of strenuous activity, the sun-filled valley is a welcome sight.

The Hersbrucker Schweiz Region

Why is this region in Middle Franconia called the Schweiz in German, the English word for Switzerland? When you think of Switzerland, high mountains and deep valleys come to mind as well as steep slopes and dark green forests in strong contrast to the snow-covered peaks - more or less a self-contained setting.

Franconia has such a landscape as well: the Hohenstein Hill with a fortress on top and the Hansgörgl Hill, the Kastental valley of the Pegnitz River between Hohenstadt and Neuhaus and the deeply cut valley of the Schwarzach River. It has well-kept forests in contrast to the rugged white malm rock on the Alb Plateau and rocky corrugated cliffs that form the walls of the valleys alongside a variety of rock formations and lookout points along the way. These are the characteristics of the Franconian Alb Plateau, better known as the Hersbrucker Schweiz, the catchment basin of the Pegnitz River. The Franconian Schweiz to the north with its various valleys is even more distinct in appearance but that region is the subject of another book!

In contrast to its northern neighbor, the Hersbrucker Schweiz is not as high and, a larger percentage of the land in the valleys has been parceled off for housing, agriculture and industrial zones that fill the extensive basins at the foothills of the region.

In the Heart of Franconia's "Switzerland"

Hersbruck, consisting of a monastery and the surrounding town belonged to a number of local noblemen including the Wittelsbach family (under Emperor Karl IV, 1360) before it became a part of the Free Imperial City of Nuremberg in 1504.

The citizens of Nuremberg built a castle that wasn't completed until 1616 by their city architect, Jakob Wolff the Younger. A three-winged construction, a popular style in the Baroque period, was complemented by two tiny stair towers, only one of which has survived.

Karst Formations

Even though the limestone layered plateaus in this region have always suffered from a lack of precipitation, the increasing amount of rainfall each year (currently over 1000 millimeters per annum) has left its mark. The lack of water is due to the porosity of the limestone that permits the precipitation to seep down through the deep fissures below. Any rock formation that is created in this way and characterized by such fissures and sinkholes is known as karst.

Thus the wide variety of scenery on the plateaus. The sinkholes themselves may be circular or oval in shape; the dry fissured valleys are often void of any outward signs of water and springs seem to appear out of nowhere in the steep stony walls where the porous limestone is covered by a layer of clay. More durable deposits of limestone created through erosion remain as rocky crags and cliffs and are ideal for rock climbing.

The seeping water causes the lime to dissolve and the fissures to widen and become caves whose roofs, through the evaporation process of the dripping water full of lime, form icicle-shaped deposits known as stalactites. The cone-shaped deposits of carbonate of lime that rise from the ground to greet the stalactites are called stalagmites. The water dripping down the walls can leave paper-thin layers of lime that resemble a lacey curtain.

Previous Pages: Hohenstein Fortress.
Left: A trip into the geological past: Maximilian Grotto, a dripstone cave near Neuhaus on the Pegnitz.
Right: A bird's eye view of the meandering Pegnitz between Hersbruck and Hohenstadt.

Cave-goers who have the urge to touch the droplets or even scrape a bit of lime off the caves should remember that removing 10 centimeters of stalactite means destroying a thousand years of work.

One of the most interesting caves open to the public is the Maximilian Grotto east of Neuhaus on the Pegnitz. The cave actually lies outside Franconia in the neighboring region of the Oberpfalz but due to the fact that access to the cave is on Franconian territory from the village of Krottensee or Toad Pond, mention is made of it here.

The Hohenstein Fortress

The highest elevation point is the Hohenstein Hill at 628 meters above sea level. The former Hohenstaufen fortress of the same name is perched on top of the rocky dolomite cliff, a position which allows it to guard the ascending Sittenbach valley from the south.

The fortress and the chapel above the gate date back to the 13th century even though the half-timbered construction makes them appear less dreary. A miniature lookout tower stands in place of a castle keep and from here the 360° view is spectacular. The hamlet of Hohenstein at the foot of the hill is Franconia's highest village.

Kirchensittenbach can boast of having one of the most charming residences of a Nuremberg patrician. The Renaissance castle was built by Wolf Jakob Stromer in 1590 for the Tetzel family. An unusual feature of the edifice consisting of numerous nooks and crannies is its domed stair tower. Currently the castle is inhabited by a distant descendent of the builder, a certain Wolfgang von Stromer.

Left: Almost in defiance of its dilapidation, Hohenstein Fortress dominates the landscape in this region due to its assertive position on top of the highest hill in the Hersbrucker Schweiz.

The Meandering Pegnitz

The word Pegnitz is derived from the Celtic word "pengerza" meaning muddy river and in Nuremberg dialect the river is still called the "Pengerz". The river breaks through the ferruginous sandstone wall and as a result, the area between Neuhaus and Hohenstadt can boast of one of the most beautiful valleys in all of Franconia. A road, a train track and the river share the narrow valley that the sturdy rock of the Jurassic Period left behind.

The river determines the contours of the valley and in the environs of Lungsdorf, including the tiny picturesque town itself, the traveler discovers one of the most romantic settings in all of Middle Franconia. Deeply-grooved rock formations accompany spectacular veins in the rocky ridges before the valley makes a sharp turn to the west beyond Hohenstadt to empty into the Rednitz on its way to the Rhine.

Now the river can take its time and meander slowly past steep and slip-off slopes as well as enchanting meadows and grassy fields on each side. Despite all its charm, the river valley, especially the lower stretches of the Pegnitz, provides sufficient space for a modest amount of farming, above all, hop-growing.

"Hops from the Hersbruck Hills" used to be a propriety article but nowadays hop-growers are far fewer in number. Yet the typical rafters and saddle roofs for drying the hops in stages discussed in the section on Spalt can be found here as well.

Veldenstein Fortress

The Veldenstein Fortress was built around the year 1480 and belonged to the bishops of Bamberg. The fortress and its distinctive keep appear overbearing to the houses of Neuhaus beneath it. The entire complex with its double line of walls, its tongue-shaped bastion extending to the north and its round watchtowers is a fine example of late medieval military architecture.

A 15th century outer bailey guards the entrance to the fortifications. The fortress, which is now privately-owned, has been turned into a hotel and restaurant and offers scenic views from the terrace and has a small zoo on the grounds.

Above: Veldenstein Fortress stretches out across the rocky spur and stands out prominently in the Pegnitz valley near Neuhaus.

From the Regnitz to the Steigerwald Wood

Gourmet Fish, Robust Wines and Noble Castles

Fish ponds sparkle in the sun and mighty fortresses dot the broad valleys between the Steigerwald Wood and the Franconian Plateau. The mirror carp raised here are enjoyed throughout Franconia. The earthy wines come from the steep vineyard slopes around the Windsheimer Bay.

Erlangen: A Blend of History and High-Tech

Erlangen, a larger city often identified with Siemens and the Friedrich-Alexander University, is located on the right bank of the Rednitz. Situated on a terrace south of the Schwabach River, which is more like a stream, the city was laid out in a large square during the age of Absolutism. Right-angled squares and street systems cut off from the daily hustle and bustle of busy traffic characterize the old part of this city. Erlangen is noted for its extensive bike paths and cyclists' right-of-way.

Twice a year the rest of Middle Franconia turns its focus on Erlangen. At Pentecost, the Bergkirchweih or hillside church dedication celebration attracts visitors from throughout the region to the Sandsteinkeller Pub of the Ratberg Hill. It is a festive event where the director of Siemens sits across the table from fellow employees and the university prof gets involved in heated discussions with his students in the shade of the old trees. Everyone drinks beer out of a stein and this lively custom unique to the region remains normally more or less civilized.

The music festival that takes place in the charming gardens of the castle around the fountain is very different in nature. The Rococo facade of the garden pavilion not only serves as the backdrop for the orchestra but also as the appropriate setting to get a glimpse of the city officials and prominent citizens of Erlangen promenading through the lush gardens.

Erlangen has always been a cosmopolitan city with its settlement of violin and other musical instrument builders in Bubenreuth. The distinguished university was founded by the margrave of Bayreuth and nowadays, Siemens, number one in medical technology, keeps Erlangen on the map.

Previous Pages: The Aischgrund countryside near Höchstadt resembles a charming mosaic due to its innumerable fish ponds that are famous for their Franconian carp.
Right: The Baroque Castle Gardens in Erlangen in full blossom; the Huguenot fountain in front of the orangery.

Culinary Coat-of-arms

What does a Middle Franconian coat-of-arms contain? It is checkered in black and white for the Ansbach-Brandenburg line, it has at least half an imperial eagle representing the imperial cities and its red and white colors stand for Franconia. The historian is fully satisfied.

The typical Franconian, however, as a gourmet has his own idea of a coat-of-arms. He conjures up "three sausages in a hard roll with mustard", thinks of tasty spareribs and would not be able to live without carp, naturally breaded and baked.

Carp from the Aischgrund Region

The Aisch River makes its way to the Regnitz between the Steigerwald Wood and the Franconian Plateau. The geological formations of the keuper hillsides are

characterized by a number of porous layers. Northeast of Neustadt the valley widens and the countryside opens up to small farms and transport routes.

Fish-breeding was especially plentiful around monasteries or bishoprics in southern Germany. In addition to the fish-breeding carried out in the Oberpfalz region, the clayey keuper plateau above the Aisch offers perfect conditions for breeding carp, formerly traditional fare during Lent.

The natural seal of the clay bed prevents precipitation from seeping further into the ground, an important consideration since the basins are fed solely by means of this precipitation and groundwater apart from the occasional flow of water from a terraced pond. The location of the shallow ponds on the edge of the Nuremberg Basin means longer hours of sunshine, which in turn influences the temperature of the water.

Although a considerable percentage of carp-breeding in Germany is carried out in the Aischgrund region, the countryside offers more than just a series of dammed up ponds. Copses of trees and farmland dot the landscape.

Nature often poses a threat. The fish in the carp beds fall prey to unwelcome guests like the cormorants and herons whose favorite hunting grounds extend all along the gleaming ribbon of water of the Main-Danube Canal. Their sheer number is a menace to the livelihood of the locals.

Fortunately, this Franconian specialty can still be found on all the regional menus during the months containing an "r". Sustained and effective carp breeding needs a break in the summer months. And the perfect ending to a pleasurable hike

Right: An ancient water scooping technique is still employed on the Regnitz near Baiersdorf where bucket water wheels are used to irrigate the fields.
Following Pages: Sunrise in the Mohrhof nature reserve in the Aischgrund region.

through the countryside around the Mohrhof dotted with fish ponds not far from Höchstadt is a visit to a regional pub serving freshly-caught, piping hot carp.

The Schwarzenberg Castle

The best view of the tremendous Schwarzenberg castle grounds near Scheinfeld is from a hot air balloon. Although it was build on the spur of a hill, the enveloping woods hide it from ordinary view.

Situated on a ridge of the Steigerwald Wood, the castle complex complete with massive round towers and battlements and outbuildings to the east dominates the hillside above the valley of one of the innumerable arms of the Aisch River.

Begun in 1610, the Catholic counts of Schwarzenberg had a early Baroque church built with yellow ornamental trim. The church faced to the south, something that was an affront to the Protestant margraves of Brandenburg. Next to the church stands the Hungerturm or Hunger Tower which has been restored to its original red hue. The origins of parts of this tower as well as the forceful square Black Tower date back to the medieval fortifications.

The southwest wing has four gables and its construction was completed by the Nuremberg city architects, Jakob Wolff and son in 1616 in the Renaissance style. The architectural plans were the creation of the famous Augsburg architect, Elias Holl.

The Schwarzenberg line of noble descent can boast a considerable amount of influence throughout Europe. Up until a few years ago, one family member was the Czech foreign minister, evidence enough of the influence and respect that the counts, who also still hold property in Bohemia, enjoy.

Left and above: The counts of Schwarzenberg have kept their castle in the family's possession since the early 17th century.

Bad Windsheim

"Bad" is the German word for spa and this spa resort enjoys an excellent reputation as such. The former free imperial city was and is the hub of the Windsheimer Bay and still competes for predominance in the region with the town of Neustadt nearby. Bad Windsheim's layout is almost circular north of the small river and is reminiscent of the days when the city was walled. This was one of the privileges the emperors granted their free imperial cities, which were also exempted from taxes.

Over the centuries, the city managed to recover time and again from being at the mercy of the power-hungry. It became a free imperial city in 1234, was later mortgaged by the emperor and then redeemed by affluent burghers. Bad Windsheim experienced the height of its power in the 16th and 17th centuries although the turbulent times of the peasant rebellions and the Thirty Years' War did not leave the city unscathed. The city was rebuilt in the Baroque style after years of war and plague only to be burned down and rebuilt in around 1730.

The average life span of a medieval city is reflected in Bad Windsheim. The Baroque Town Hall, built on one of the many gypsum hills in the Windsheimer Bay, can be seen from far and wide. Several patrician buildings dating from the Renaissance and the Rococo periods give testimony to the wealth of the proud inhabitants. Small modest quarters in the Spitalgasse Street were the homes and workplaces of craftsmen and farmers.

Living History

Bad Windsheim's major attraction is its Open Air Museum, probably one of the most interesting in all of Germany. Typically Franconian farmsteads have found

Left: Typical farmhouse and blacksmith's, rebuilt in its entirety in the Open Air Museum in Bad Windsheim.

a new home here after having fallen into disrepair in their original locations. Each stone, each board was carefully numbered before bringing them to this idyllic setting where they were carefully restored to their original functions. Farmhouses and craftsmen's abodes, historical mills, pubs and shepherds' cottages have been reassembled in enclaves according to region or epoch.

Special craft demonstrations presented by professionals in authentic costumes at the individual farmsteads bring the museum to life. Threshing and weaving by hand, juice-making, beer brewing and wood-fire baking as well ox-drawn or horse-drawn plows in the fields all contribute to making this a memorable museum.

Captured Sunshine

The average Middle Franconian likes what he's used to and that applies to his drinking habits as well. Middle and Upper Franconians are beer drinkers even when they happen to live next to tasty grapes growing on the next clay slope.

The former steep vineyard slopes were, in part, flattened and then consolidated and are now accessible to the hiker via asphalt paths all year round. Autumn is an espe-

cially beautiful time of year to ramble through the vineyards: the air is crisp and clear and affords lovely views of the village of Markt Ipsheim and the Town Hall tower of Bad Windsheim.

Riesling, Silvaner and Müller-Thurgau as well as Bachus and Kerner appellations grow in the loamy soil. The friendly wine-growers and wine inns in the area offer a wide selection of local wines served with hot onion cake. Red wines are beginning to gain a foothold on the market as well and Blauburgunder, Domina and Dornfelder wines are worth trying. Wine-growers from Ipsheim even offer their wines in the vineyards on the weekends.

The Hoheneck Fortress

The refurbished fortress offers a superb view of the surrounding countryside. Its successful conversion makes it all the more difficult to realize the important role this proud edifice played in its stormy history.

The medieval fortress changed owners several times: first it would be plundered only then to be treated with the best of care, all due to its strategic position. The entire Aischgrund Region and, in particular the area around Windsheim, was the object of ardent desire to the margraves of Ansbach, the prince-bishop of Würzburg, the burgrave of Nuremberg and the various monasteries. Here the blessings of a bishop or abbot were just as common as the consternation of land struggles.

Left: Two half-timbered houses were rebuild here stone by stone in the Bad Windsheim Open Air Museum (wine-grower's house and farmhouse).
Above: An authentic wine-grower's winepress in the museum.
Following Pages: The wine grown in Middle Franconia is nothing to be ashamed of: the best slopes are those below Hoheneck Fortress near Ipsheim.

Festive City with a Palace and Castles Dotting the Hillsides

Once the home of influential margraves, the region and its capital now pride themselves in the stately homes of the local nobility and Rococo castles.

Onolzbach now Ansbach

The inhabitants of Ansbach never had an easy time of it when confronted with the mockery of the free imperial cities. Even though its margraves had to share their power over the Rangau Region with other local nobility, these margraves will be remembered for creating Franconia's Rococo City.

Ansbach, the district capital of Middle Franconia, was founded by a nobleman named Gumbert who in the eighth century had a monastery built on the spot where the Onolzbach Stream flows into the Rezat River. Today, St. Gumbert's Church with its three mighty and rather unusual towers is a reminder of the city's beginnings.

The name Onolzbach for Ansbach remained a part of the official administrative records until the 18th century. The city had been the residential seat of the Brandenburg-Onolzbach princes since 1456. The Hohenzollern dynasty had previously acquired the city in 1331 at a time when the citizens were dreaming of turning their city into an independent imperial one just like its surrounding neighbors.

Previous Pages: *Beringershof, Ansbach's most beautiful courtyard directly behind St. Gumbert's Church. The windows of the 16th century spiral staircase follow the stairs as they wind upward.*
Left: *The unique setting for the weekly market is between St. Gumbert's and the Castle.*
Below: *"Anscavallo", Jürgen Goertz's modern sculpture on the Schlossplatz was the topic of many a heated discussion among the inhabitants of Ansbach.*

The Old Town

The cityscape of Ansbach reveals a number of varying architectural styles. The medieval center, unlike other Franconian towns dominated by half-timbered buildings, exhibits a large number of stucco facades. One of the lovelier examples is snugly set beneath the towers of St. Gumbert's: the Haus der Landstädte, which once served as the courthouse for the burgraves of Nuremberg.

The more patrician part of the medieval city, which was walled in the Middle Ages, lies to the southwest. The charming 15th and 16th century facades were refurbished in the late Baroque period of the 18th century and the uneven spires of St. John's Parish Church loom over this part of the old city.

The City of Margraves

The Castle as it stands today is a product of the 18th century and is most likely the reason that Ansbach is known as the "Rococo City of Franconia". The ingenious architect, Gabriel de Gabrieli, was already well-known in Franconia for his perfectly-proportioned facades in the town of Eichstätt. The citizens of nearby Windsheim had their Town Hall built with the expressed intent of outdoing the castle in Ansbach, something that barely bothered the Baroque craftsman de Gabrieli.

The Castle has a number of showcase rooms which are used on ceremonial occasions but the majority of the 500 rooms houses the Middle Franconian government offices. The well-planned infrastructure outside the medieval city is practical

Far left: The splendid embodiment of the Rococo era: the Cabinet of Mirrors in the Castle. The reflection of the mirrors makes the dimensions of the room seem endless.
Left: Ansbach has made a name for itself in all corners of the globe through its manufacture of faience and porcelain. Venus and Mercury are just two examples on display in the museum.
Above: A Meißner porcelain clock in the margrave's Castle.

and convenient and does not detract from the character of Ansbach, one of most delightful Hohenzollern cities in southern Germany.

The Ansbach internet pages recommend a guided tour through the 27 stately apartments of the palace. Especially noteworthy is the two-storey Festive Hall and the Cabinet of Mirrors as well as the Tile Hall where 2800 tiles from the former court manufacturer in Ansbach are on display.

Above: The "Margrave's Festival" in front of the orangery in the courtyard gardens is one of the cultural highlights of the annual Rococo theater performances.
Right: Falconry demonstration during the annual festivities.

The Bavarian State Collection of faience and porcelain is on exhibit on the ground floor. This magnificent collection extends far beyond local production and is a must for porcelain lovers.

The Days at Court Come Alive

The splendor of the Castle serves as the backdrop for the Rococo Festival held at the beginning of July each summer. Locals dress up in authentic 17th and 18th century costumes complete in every detail down to the powder, perfume and wigs and perform delicate dance steps to Rococo music. Life at the margrave-Brandenburg court comes alive throughout the Castle and in the court gardens in front of the orangery. The entire city proudly celebrates its cultural heritage.

Kasper Hauser in Ansbach

The relations between the Ansbach-Brandenburg margraves and the German princes took on a strange twist with the appearance of a certain Kasper Hauser, to whom a fountain in Ansbach is dedicated. He was captured on the Unschlitt Square in 1828 in Nuremberg where he told a marvelous tale of how he had been imprisoned in a dark dungeon for years on end and therefore knew nothing of his origin.

The tale turned into a criminal case five years later when he was discovered stabbed to death in the castle gardens of Ansbach. Rumors and speculations surrounding this foundling still abound today and no one has ever been able determine his family line for certain. Perhaps he was of princely blood but illegitimate and thus an undesirable heir to the princes of Baden. Modern-day investigations have analyzed the blood found on his underwear and DNA analyses have been made on his hair. The dilapidated cellar vault of the Pilsach Castle ruin near Neumarkt and a secret dungeon in the Beuggen Castle on the Rhine have also been carefully scrutinized but no definitive answers have been found.

The Bureau of Tourist Information in Ansbach has profited from this unsolved mystery. The city is the venue of numerous seminars and memorial ceremonies and the ongoing interest in the enigmatic Kasper Hauser lends a tad of madness to this pretty but sleepy administrative city.

Right: Sidewalk cafe at the entrance to the Old Town in front of the Herrieder Gate.
Below: The Löwengrube building dates back to 1566 and successfully incorporates half-timbers and stone adornment in its facade.

FOTO-HELZEL
BERNING
Cafe
SCHNEIDER WEISSE

Worthwhile Day Trips

Not all the tourist sights in the environs of the residential city of Ansbach, however, can be attributed to the margraves.

Some of the most bitter foes of the margraves resided in an exclave, the Imperial City of Nuremberg, just a few kilometers down the Rezat. Today the medieval walls surrounding the Old Town of Nuremberg remind one of a miniature town, an offshoot of the former imperial city.

Lichtenau was also a real thorn in the flesh of the margrave holdings. The defiant fortress the citizens of Nuremberg built to protect themselves from their own former burgraves is star-shaped and considered to be one of the best preserved Renaissance fortifications in Germany.

Colmberg Fortress

The country road from Ansbach to Rothenburg crosses the watershed and dips into the broad upper Altmühl valley. Colmberg Fortress is perched on a hillside above the town bearing the same name. Once imperial fortifications, the fortress is built of large porous sandstone blocks still bearing the marks of the tongs that moved them into place.

A bit of world history is recorded within the walls of this fortress. The economically unsuccessful counts of Truhending were replaced by the burgraves of Nuremberg from whose line Frederick VI descended. Frederick served under King Sigismund in Hungary in the early 15th

Above: Cadolzburg Fortress was once the principal estate of the burgraves of Nuremberg.
Below: Colmberg Fortress, formerly an abbey chapel whose foundations date back to the 13th century.

century and as a result of his loyalty was given Mark Brandenburg as a fief.

The curtain wall still contains some of the original battlements and the Romanesque palace in the southern tract houses a pillared hall on the ground floor. The round castle keep built of blocks of bossed stone towers over the entire complex which has been successfully converted into a very picturesque hotel that is ideal for family gatherings and festivities.

The Hohenzollern Family Fortress

Around 1200 Cadolzburg Fortress along with Abenberg Fortress went to the burgraves of Nuremberg and was to be their main residence for the following centuries. The Hohenzollern family maintained their burgrave castle in Nuremberg until the early 15th century when they moved to the more comfortable and safer Cadolzburg.

The complex stands precipitously when viewed from the west. Its romantic entrance is from the oldest part of the town of Cadolzburg. Although there is no evident castle keep, the fortress shares a number of architectural similarities with Abenberg. Cadolzburg is considered one

of the best preserved fortresses of a dynasty still in existence.

The Second World War caused severe bomb damage but wonderful restoration work has been carried over the past decades. The fortress is to be used as a branch of the Bavarian Archives or as a fortress museum.

The Crailsheim Family

The lords von Eyb, a powerful family in Franconia but an especially powerful line of counts in the Rangau region, resided in Sommersdorf. As vassals of the bishop of Eichstätt, they had a square moated castle built around 1400. The curtain wall with a series of bastions surrounds the castle that consists of two parallel tracts.

The castle has been in the Crailsheim family since 1550 and distant relatives still reside there. The lords of Crailsheim brought the Reformation to Sommersdorf and expanded their holdings through purchases and bequests.

Heilsbronn on the Franconian Pilgrims' Path

Heilsbronn is a station along a German section of the Pilgrims' Path that leads from Hersbruck via Nuremberg to Rothenburg and continues into Swabia. The former Cistercian abbey has been a part of the town's history for four centuries and the former Minster is atypical for the architecture of this order: it is a combination of an impressive Romanesque interior intertwined with elegant Gothic additions.

Left: The moated castle in Sommersdorf, just west of Triesdorf, is said to be the birthplace of the humanist and author, Albrecht von Eyb (1420-1475).
Below: The Minster in Heilsbronn displaying the sarcophagi of the Hohenzollern family.

A History Lesson Evolving Around Water and Beer

The good life: where sailing masts and hop poles compete and Celtic and Roman history goes hand in hand with modern-day tourism.

The Newly-created Plateau of Lakes

When a Middle Franconian gets out his swimming suit, he is probably not heading off to one of the local swimming pools despite the fact that they are fully-equipped with breath-taking waterslides. It is one of the lakes between the Altmühl and the Rezat rivers that he is most likely to be heading to, some veritable competition for the sterile, city-run pools. These lakes are not only frequented by the Middle Franconians, in the meantime, they have become centers of leisure time activities for all of southern Germany. Easy access to swimming in sparkling clean lakes and relaxing on sandy strips of beach as well as quality campgrounds attract numerous tourists.

A few comparisons to the lakes in southern Bavaria may be of use here. The Altmühl Lake is 450 hectares and thus almost as large as the Königssee. The Roth Lake is 220 hectares and thus about the size of the Schliersee while the Brombach Lake (1270 hectares) is larger than the Tegernsee.

At first glance, the Altmühl Lake, the Igelsbach-Vorsperre Lake, the Brombach Lakes as well as Roth Lake, all seem to be a result of superb citizen-oriented local planning in an economically-depressed region. These lakes are, however, part and parcel of a gigantic transfer of water.

Water for Northern Bavaria

Northern Bavaria, of which Middle Franconia is a part, suffers from a lack of water since the surroundings hillsides only receive around a third of the precipitation that the rivers of the Alps south of the Danube are accustomed to. In the past, dry summers meant getting drinking water from supply tanks and cities and industries were forced to cut back drastically in their consumption of water. The ground water was full of agricultural pollutants that flowed into the rivers and the rivers were so low that they could no longer cleanse themselves.

A New Natural Habitat

The technicians involved in this extensive construction of a canal and numerous lakes demanded a lot from the surrounding countryside. Eviscerated by flooding and squandered in part as depleted sand quarries, valuable inhabitable land was desecrated and the inhabitants were forced to adapt to the fact that their quiet country roads would be packed with tourists. Fauna and flora had to be replanted and restored and a ecological balance attained. Most important of all was the restitution of a quality of life to the inhabitants between Gunzenhausen, Spalt and Weißenburg.

The Vogelinsel or Bird Island in the northern part of the Altmühl Lake is one of

Previous pages: An artificial landscape has been created: the Brombachvorsperre, a dammed-up lake in a part of the Franconian plateau of lakes.
Left: Yachts docked at the Brombach Lake.
Above: A sailing and surfing paradise that even attracts water sport enthusiasts from Upper Bavaria.
Following pages: The Vogelinsel Nature Reserve in the Altmühl Lake provides a sheltered habitat and breeding grounds for rare waterfowl from near and far.

these contributions to nature. Rare birds nest here, small animals find refuge and various species of amphibians inhabit this part of the lake. A planked footpath allows the nature lover to explore this nature reserve along designated paths. Information plaques and guided tours help ensure that the pristine conditions of the island can be maintained and preserved.

The City and its Hops: Spalt

After you have enjoyed sailing on the Altmühl Lake, hiked along the small canals Überleiter Ost and West across the watershed, had a swim in the Brombach Lake and satisfied your culinary desires in one

of the innumerable restaurants around the lakes, you are ready for a visit to Spalt.

This small town has much to offer. Although the Rezat River makes a deep cut into the crumbly keuper soil, there is still room for extensive hop-growing. The vines' supporting poles are up to six meters tall and amply protected from the wind in the sandy basins of the valleys. The soil is ideal for these fragile plants.

Alongside the Hallertau, the Franconian Jura and the Hersbruck Hills, the hop-growing region around Spalt has the best of Bavaria's cultivable hop-growing soil at its disposal. The hops grown near Spalt, however, deserve special mention since these hops have a delightful earthy aroma that enhances beer and is renowned around the world.

Hop sprout salad is a specialty of the pubs in Spalt at the beginning of April each year when the first sprouts break through the soil in far greater number than can climb the poles and survive.

The Mühlreisighaus on the west side of Spalt is Germany's most unique example of a hop-drying hall. The precious fruit was transported through a series of five sieves, depending on the phase of dryness from the upper floor of the gable downwards in order to release the resinous powder, lu-

Left: The multi-storied hops building provided enough space for drying in the Spalt region. One of the best examples is the Mühlreisighaus between Spalt and Wassermungenau.
Below: The aromatic umbellate hop blossoms.

pulin, from the strobiles of the plant. Just a tad was needed to give beer an earthy taste and a pinch of it served as a sedative.

Aside from the churches, the most distinctive feature of the countryside is the old buildings that were all erected in a similar style using similar building materials for economic reasons. In this hop-growing region, the unusual rafters and the numerous slots in the roofs stand out. Traditionally, the hops were dried in the gables on individual floors made evident by the rows of windows in the saddle roofs. Nowadays modern drying techniques keep the air temperature constant.

How long can the hop-growing industry survive in this ideal setting? Forecasts are not favorable due to fluctuating prices on the global market, competition from abroad, especially from Central Europe, and the eastward expansion of the European Union. Moreover, this time-intensive work from planting to harvest, despite the assistance of modern technology, is becoming a dying art. Fewer and fewer young people are willing to take up the trade.

Residences of the Local Nobility

Several romantic fortresses and castles are concealed in the foothills of the Franconian Alb near Roth and its environs. These are relics of former monasteries or homes of greater or lesser noble lords. Abenberg Fortress and Sandsee Castle near Pleinfeld are just two examples.

Abenberg Fortress

One of the most strategically-important 11th and 12th century fortifications has

Left: The so-called Scottish Tower of the Abenberg Fortress.
Below: Sandsee Castle near Pleinfeld: a 12-meter high ring wall almost completely surrounds this late 12th century complex.

survived and is now one of Middle Franconia's loveliest fortress settings. The Hohenzollern family, the burgraves of Nuremberg, inherited the lands of the Abenberg family around 1200 and expanded the fortress to its current size.

It didn't take long until the fortress came under the guardianship of the bishop of Eichstätt in whose possession it remained until 1766. It was sold in 1796 to the Prussian-Ansbach family and then annexed to the state of Bavaria in 1806. After that, the fortress changed hands several times and its owners distinguished themselves by neglecting the complex. Today, the bailey does seem extremely barren and atypical of the fortresses in Franconia that normally had a palace and castle keep in their center.

In 1875 a Munich art historian began renovating the castle. Many buildings constructed in the last quarter of the 19th century were built to resemble the medieval edifices of the well-to-do. Thus the refurbished Scottish Tower now resembles the Nassauer House in Nuremberg. A round water trough rebuilt in the middle of the bailey has long since been removed and with it most certainly historical material that could reveal some close links to the fortress's past.

Wernfels Fortress

Wernfels Fortress, resting on the spur of the hill, looks down on the Franconian Rezat. The fortifications originally belonged to a family of estate officials and later they were owned by a well-known patrician family in Nuremberg. The fortress was erected in 1250 and enlarged and modernized to a comfortable Renaissance palace in 1600. Some of the refinements are still evident in the palace that has meanwhile been turned into a Youth Education Center. Although the fortress no longer can be visited, a trip to the top of the promontory is worth the effort for a panoramic view of the countryside including the Abenberg Fortress in the distance.

Although the bishops of Eichstätt were largely responsible for the castle's current appearance, several architectural traits of an earlier era are evident. There are two Gothic gatehouses and the north flank of the palace itself reveals the fortified character common in the Hohenstaufen era.

The Wülzburg Fortress Threatens the Imperial City

The peace-loving Benedictines settled on a spur of the southern Franconian Alb in the 11th century. Following the Reformation, they were forced to yield their land to the margraves of Ansbach who had Georg and Blasius Berwart construct highly-modern star-shaped Renaissance fortifications. The sole purpose of this fortress

Left: Wernfels Fortress was first documented in 1197 and is now used a youth hostile and Protestant youth center.
Below: The stately fortifications of the Wülzburg above Weißenburg. Here the margraves of Ansbach clearly demonstrated their borders to the burghers of the free imperial city.

was to force the burghers of Weißenburg to respect the margraves' power. In the end, however, the intimidated inhabitants did triumph. In 1882 the city of Weißenburg purchased the entire complex and a visit to the pleasantly-renovated fortifications is worthwhile.

Weißenburg and the Roman Baths

The district city of Weißenburg is one of the gems in a series of towns that run along the Roman frontier fortifications of the Limes. Two thousand years ago the Romans set up their wall of defense complete with ditches and palisades to protect themselves from what they considered to be savage German tribes. The wall was guarded by a series of watchtowers which were insufficient in number to truly be effective.

The early settlement of Castrum Biricianis on the spur was of major strategic importance since from here easy access to the Danube could be controlled.

As so often is the case, the royal settlement of Weißenburg near the Gothic Andreas Church became the site of the future imperial city. The city's layout becomes evident where the two main streets cross at the Town Hall. Portions of the medieval wall and ditch and pond have survived along with a large number of half-timbered buildings.

In the past few years the Roman baths nearby have been excavated and investigated bit by bit and are now protected from wind and weather by an extensive roof. Yet the watchtower near Weißenburg as well as the baths near Theilenhofen are a mere fragment of the Roman culture in the border strip between the German and the Celtic tribes. Further

Left: One of the most exquisite and well-known city gates in Franconia: The 14th century Ellinger Gate in Weißenburg symbolizes the city's successful rise to a free imperial city.
Following pages: The pond wall is a part of Weißenburg's city fortifications.

clues are more readily revealed by aerial photography: specially-designed cameras help reconstruct the outlines of ancient settlements in farmers' fields.

A Popular Stamp Motif

A portion of Weißenburg's medieval walls still surround the Old Town. The main street that runs from south to north leaves the city behind through the highly-decorative Ellinger Gate, one of the most beautiful Romanesque sandstone gates in Germany and thus a popular stamp motif. A few kilometers further north lies the town of Ellingen, known as the "Pearl of Franconian Baroque".

Weißenburg's reputation stems from the magnificent 13th century castle built by the Knights of the Teutonic Order. It was originally a moated castle that Margrave Albrecht Alcibiades destroyed in 1552 during the Second Margrave War. The

castle was later rebuilt in the Renaissance style consisting of three wings flanked by a Gothic church on the north side to enclose a square inner courtyard. Between 1708-1721 the castle was refurbished in the Baroque style.

The spectacular staircase in the middle pavilion, Joseph Anton Roth's stucco work and Johann Anton Pinck's ceiling fresco of the "Battle of the Gods versus the Titans" provide some superb examples of the opulence and splendor that were so popular during this era. The Castle Church as well was renovated in the 18th century and a vaulted ceiling inserted and the church redecorated in the Baroque style. The careful observer can still detect the high Gothic windows of the original church.

The Knights of the Teutonic Order

Nowadays the enormous amount of influence and power that the Knights of the Teutonic Order enjoyed in the High Middle Ages can hardly be imagined; at best the Order can be documented in the architectural remnants we are fortunate to still have. After the Order returned from the eastern regions, it made Bad Mergentheim its center but the next higher tier in the hierarchy in the district of Franconia chose Ellingen as its seat. Other remnants of the Order can be found in Nuremberg between St. Elizabeth's and St. John's as well as in Dinkelsbühl or in Virnsberg where there is a castle and a hall.

Every establishment of the Order was vested with extensive powers and land, sometimes intertwined with complicated ownership rights and right of use. Nowadays the Teutonic Order cannot carry out its work without making use of state subsidies and various tax breaks.

Left: Roman heritage: the Nuremberg architect, Mr. Wörrlein, designed the protective roof for the excavated baths.
Above: Two Roman artifacts on display in the Roman Museum in Weißenburg.

The Fossa Carolina

Charlemagne's geometricians were perfectly right in 793 when they discovered near the town of Graben what they thought was the deep connection across the watershed between the Main River and thus the Rhine river system in the north and the Danube river system in the south. Not much remains of this early attempt to fulfill an ancient dream of building a connection between the North Sea and the Black Sea.

The lower Altmühl Valley begins at the town of Treuchtlingen, which lies at the foot of a fortress ruin. Here box-shaped valleys and steep rocky cliffs formed in the Jurassic Period dominate the landscape. Field Marshall Georg Heinrich Graf von Pappenheim, an historical figure in Friedrich Schiller's play "Wallenstein", was born here in 1574. His family fortress stood a few kilometers further down the river in the village of Pappenheim. This romantic ruin is a culmination of several centuries of construction - for example, the two protruding round

Left: The marvelous front facade of the castle of the Knights of the Teutonic Order in Ellingen is considered to be the gem of Franconian Baroque.
Below: "Drutelinga" Castle used to belong to the local nobility and knights of Treuchtlingen.
Following pages: Pappenheim Fortress, situated high above the Altmühl valley, has been a ruin since the Thirty Years' War.

towers are sophisticated examples of 16th century defense technology.

The Watershed Plateau

There are four hamlets on the plateau of the Franconian Alb south of Weißenburg that are worth a detour. Göhren is one of them. These are southern Germany's sole examples of villages set up around a meadow or oval-shaped common. The church and a quenching pond as well as grass for sheep-grazing are all a part of this common green encompassed by two access roads.

Theses villages have also maintained some of the original farm houses that are indigenous to this karst region. Their heavy limestone slated roofs are flatter than usual due to the weight they bear. The stone slabs are from nearby stone quarries that export thin layers of limestone around the world. The region is an Eldorado for fossil collectors looking for ammonite, belemnite and fossilized sea snails and shells from the Jurassic Period.

A Home for an Extinct Bird

It would be presumptuous to assume that a hobby collector could come across a second archaeopteryx, an extinct reptile-like bird of the Jurassic Period. After a contentious discussion as to its authenticity, the fossil molds are now on display in the Jurassic Museum in Eichstätt. This museum is truly unique. Its implementation of modern of technology offers informative displays that enable visitors of all ages to be fascinated by the varying geological structures found in the Altmühl Valley.

Left: World-famous fossil: an archaeopteryx.
Above: Much sought-after limestone slabs are quarried outside Solnhofen.

Ancient Settlements

The high range of hills that form the southern border of the broad Altmühl Valley are full of ancient settlements. The Sueben entrenchment on the Gelbe Burg as well as the Spielberg Fortress with the Hahnenkamm Range as a backdrop both stand out prominently. Nowadays regional culinary specialties, artifacts, and open air theaters make this a noteworthy region.

The River Flows Uphill

The European Watershed between Treuchtlingen and Pappenheim is peaceful and quiet. Its geological surroundings, however, have been undergoing changes for several million years now and the Altmühl and the Rezat rivers have played a major role.

The Main River that bends to the northwest by Bamberg and heads for the Rhine past Schweinfurt and Würzburg had a predecessor, the Old Main. This river though, never considered making a bend by Bamberg. Instead, it headed through the Rednitz Basin straight south, broke through the valley watershed in which Charlemagne had his Fossa Carolina built and flowed into a wider river near Solnhofen, which had formed an enormous valley in the direction of Eichstätt, Beilngries and Kelheim.

An ancient predecessor of the Danube that made its way through the dry valley near Wellheim to the Altmühl was responsible for a valley much too wide for the narrow Altmühl. The erosion caused by the Old Danube was also responsible for the splendid limestone reef deposits that the Jurassic period left behind.

Technical Challenges

The newly-created plateau of lakes can, at best, transfer only one-fifth of the water supply necessary for northern Bavaria. The new Main-Danube Canal bears the main load.

Water is pumped from southern Bavaria to the north from the Altmühl in Dietfurt and from the Danube in Kehlheim and then transferred via giant sluices across the European watershed between the Danube and the Rhine. The fact that this water transfer doubles as one of the largest navigation routes in Germany is certainly a positive by-product for this economically weak region with a dwindling population density.

The octogenarian farmers have a right to shake their heads in doubt when they cast a glance at the wide ribbon of water flowing high above the Altmühl valley and ask themselves if the water has begun flowing up the hill. It flows upwards to Roth Lake where the water from the Europa Canal is stored at the summit until it is needed. Roth Lake appropriately serves as a reservoir as well as a recreational facility for bathers and surfers alike. It is then released via the Kleine Roth River to the Rednitz or via the north ramp and its locks in the direction of the Main River.

Left and above: Spielberg Castle, south of Gunzenhausen, is the home and workplace of the contemporary sculptor and painter, Ernst Steinacker.
Following pages: Hoarfrost in the Altmühl valley.

Varying Water Levels

Swimming is not always that safe near the outlet of the Main-Danube Canal since the undercurrent below the canal up to the Small Roth Lake and continuing on to the Rednitz River can be immense. The water level of the lake is constantly changing.

Yet this phenomenon is nothing new to the region. In fact, a typical characteristic of the Altmühl River was its ever-varying water level. Flooding used to be quite common and valuable soil being carried away as well as crop devastation and swampy fields were the consequences.

The plight of the farmer and landowner before the creation of the Altmühl Lake was a surplus of water. Now, after its creation, the farmer observes sinking groundwater levels and a depletion of certain types of vegetation and microorganisms.

Right: The Twelve Disciples, limestone reef from the Jurassic Period when this area east of Solnhofen was under water.

Medieval German Towns: A Walk into the Past

The former free imperial cities lie picturesquely nestled in the countryside. They have managed to maintain their medieval character and are thus some of the most popular tourist sights in all of Germany.

GASTHOF

„La Isla'

The Romantic Road

The Romantic Road leads from Würzburg via Rothenburg, Feuchtwangen, Dinkelsbühl, Nördlingen and Augsburg south to Italy. The road follows the natural line across the high plateaus of shell limestone and in Middle Franconia, it follows the ascent to the Frankenhöhe Plateau. A closer look at the map makes it clear that the cities along this route did not arbitrarily join together; this north-south route that was of such importance in the Middle Ages still performs a necessary function today.

Small wonder that the cities along this Romantic Road developed into major players in the 13th and 14th centuries and worked their way up to the status of imperial free cities. The traveler might, at times, have a hard time keeping in mind the concept "romantic". The charming cityscapes and rolling hills of the countryside often stand counterpoint to the weak infrastructure and economic disadvantages in this part of Middle Franconia. It is thus all the more understandable that the tourist industry is essential to the economic survival of the towns in the region.

Rothenburg ob der Tauber

Rothenburg ob der Tauber (above the Tauber), however, never fails to please its visitors. The view from the west from the bed of the Tauber River up the steep vine–yard slopes to the medieval rooftops and towers soaring above has been compared to a view of Jerusalem.

Page 120: Rothenburg's unique medieval cityscape from the west.
Previous pages: Just one of the numerous romantic settings in Rothenburg: the Plönlein.
Below: "Silent Night" at the Gerlach-smithy in Rothenburg.
Right: The Markus Tower and Röder Arch are a part of the second city wall.
Following pages: The Town Hall at the Market Place in Rothenburg. This is the quintessence of the German Romantic to many tourists.

HOTEL MARKUS TURM
RES

IEN-APOTHEKE

The Hohenstaufen dynasty began setting up a town on the site of an earlier fortress belonging to the counts of Kochergau. Rothenburg soon became a piece in the mosaic of territorial politics in southern Germany, a desired object of all the descendents of the Hohenstaufen dynasty. Rudolf of Hapsburg issued a letter of freedom that in exchange for loyalty and services to the Holy Roman Empire prevented the local nobility from interfering in city affairs.

As in most free imperial cities, the ministerial officials became the ruling families, later known as patricians. Over time the city council was forced to expand to incorporate the growing number of burghers and craftsmen. Clever tactics permitted Rothenburg to have an enormous territorial influence on the surrounding area. This influence served two purposes: on the one hand, the land outside the fortified city was very fertile and on the other hand, the farmers in the surrounding countryside were ensured of making a small fortune from their crops.

An Influential Mayor

One of these farmers, Heinrich Toppler, turned out to be one of the leading men in the city. As mayor during the turbulent times before and after 1400, he successfully managed to run the city, naturally without neglecting his personal interests as well. His own choice in marriage as well as the proper choices of partners from the patrician families in Nuremberg, Dinkelsbühl and Nördlingen for his children secured his power. Toppler eventually became the commander of the troops in the Swabian League, a league that was opposed to the local nobility.

After Toppler's death in 1408, his descendents were deprived of their power and the city government established itself as democratic form of rule. The increasing influence of its burghers and craftsmen in the development of the city over the centuries has allowed Rothenburg to retain its unique medieval appearance and charm.

The City Spreads Out

City development between the 13th and the 16th centuries becomes evident by walking through the narrow streets past the city's towers. The Weißer Turm or

White Tower and the Markus Tower date back to the first enclosure while the Spital, Röder and Würzburg Towers were a part of the second and final medieval wall in the east on which the bastion and a charitable foundation project along the spur of the hill to the south of the city.

The idyllic setting, the medieval buildings and their inhabitants interspersed among the large number of churches and monasteries impressed artists and literary writers alike at the beginning of the 19th century. The fascination for this city as a work of art seemed contagious. Much of

Above: 13th/14th century convent kitchen of the Dominican nuns now in the Reichsstadt Museum.

this fascination has characterized the way the locals feel about their town.

Although many a leading family moved elsewhere at the end of the period of imperial cities, a glance at the street signs and building names remind both the visitor and the locals of Rothenburg's glorious past. Even the new suburbs outside Rothenburg maintain a respectful distance to the medieval city center.

Local Inhabitants Help Preserve their History

And, Rothenburg has to make the most of its historical past. When the state bor-

der to Württemberg was created to the west of the city, expansion in that direction became impossible. Jobs that were generously subsidized by the state also disappeared.

The tourist industry, nevertheless, continues to boom. Every tourist from abroad needs to include Rothenburg on his list of must-sees in Germany. The kaleido-

scope of impressions is endless: stores selling Christmas ornaments and wooden pyramids all year round, tourists lugging video cams, the highest water consumption at one in the morning when Asian tourists head once more for the bathtubs, interesting museums and crowded narrow streets. The city is well in the hands of its local inhabitants, a lively place chock full of sights.

Especially around Pentecost, memories of the free imperial city reawaken each year

Left: A Baroque statue in the fortress gardens in Rothenburg.
Above: The might bastion at the Spital Gate was a part of the final phase of city's fortification.
Following pages: The scene of the Last Supper on the Holy Blood Altar by Tilman Riemenschneider in St. Jacob's Parish Church in Rothenburg.

when the inhabitants of the city put on an historical play surrounding the events of the Thirty Years' War (1618-1648). According to a legend by the glassblower and poet, Adam Hörber, a former mayor by the name of Nusch saved the free imperial city from destruction by the commander of the army of the Catholic League, Tilly, in 1631 by drinking a pitcher containing the equivalent of 13 glasses of wine in one swallow in front of the commander.

Rumor has it that not a few tourists from abroad attempt to reenact this praiseworthy example set by the former Mayor Nusch. And believe it or not - the city still stands. Moreover, the city must prove time and again that it can withstand the quakes of fireworks and flares that cause the medieval walls to shake during the performances of historical plays.

The Hohenlohe Family at Schillingsfürst

Of the four major rivers whose well-heads are just a few kilometers from one another in western Middle Franconia, the Wörnitz is the most southerly. Upstream, the Würzburg-Ulm highway has accompanied the river for several years and the river flows parallel to the Romantic Road between Rothenburg and Nördlingen.

Near the Feuchtwangen highway interchange and north of the well-head of the Wörnitz lies the town of Schillingsfürst at the foot of the Franconian Plateau. A Baroque castle belonging to the Hohenlohe family whose authority extended this far was built atop the hill in 1724. The castle is a typical three-winged construction decorated with vertical pillars. In the central wing, the pillars extend above the portal to join an oval gable.

Stucco ceilings and paneling as well as projecting staircases and ostentatious apartments make up the interior while statues representing the four seasons adorn the gardens. The water tower with its unique pumping system, however, is

what gives this castle a particular notoriety. An ox was given the unpleasant task of continuously ascending the slightly slanted wooden plank axis in the center of the tower in order to keep the water supply flowing into the deep castle well.

The castle replaced a 12th century fortress that was destroyed during the Thirty Years' War. An arched stone bridge leads across the former moat into the castle. Falconry demonstrations on the spur of the hill are a special treat in this ideal setting.

In the town of Schillingfürst itself, an unusual dialect, a type of thieves' Latin, has been preserved down to the present. Market ladies and traveling peddlers still speak a tongue that is reminiscent of the days of servants in court households. The secret signs and symbols, easily understood by those in-the-know, present the linguist with an entirely new world of research.

A Varied Countryside

The typical Franconian countryside abounds in a variety of crops and vegetation. Whereas in other regions where the consolidation of landholdings resulted in large portions of land being cleared and thus made less economically-viable, in the Ansbach region, great pains were taken to set up fields with hedged borders

Above: Schillingsfürst Castle has been owned by the counts of Hohenlohe since 1313.

and to maintain farm tracks and irrigation ditches. This careful attention to detail has paid off.

Refurbishing the villages has also been successful especially in western Middle Franconia. The quality of rural life has been immensely improved through the implementation of useful building measures: renewing sidewalks and providing turnaround routes for farm machinery. Häslabronn and Lehrberg are just two good examples.

Feuchtwangen and its Cloister Performances

The situation was entirely different from Rothenburg in the former free imperial city

of Feuchtwangen. Its humble beginnings were a Benedictine abbey and although the city received its imperial status in the 13th century, it was not until 1395 that the city was completely walled in. Only one of the three former gates to the city remains, the Obertor or Upper Gate.

The town abounds with half-timbered buildings and two very different spires ascend from the Stiftskirche (church) north of the Market Square while the remnants of the original Benedictine abbey still manage to characterize the town. The Romanesque cloister of the abbey with its half-timbered upper story doesn't only serve as a tourist attraction, it also provides the enchanting stage setting for the well-known Kreuzgangspiele or Cloister Plays held each summer.

Feuchtwangen is going through a process of change, in part due to its easy access to the Nuremberg-Heilbronn and Würzburg-Ulm highways nearby. It is becoming a service-oriented city for the entire region. The addition of a casino also makes the city more attractive.

Left: The late Romanesque cloister and garden provide the ideal backdrop for the Cloister Plays held here each summer.
Above: The Stiftskirche (church) is a part of the former abbey complex.

The Imperial City of Dinkelsbühl

It would be nice if the city's crest featuring a chaff of spelt or Dinkel in German, had actually taken its name from the spelt growing on the hill beyond the town. Scholars claim that the city's name was first documented in 1188 by Frederick Barbarossa and that it was originally Dingolf or Dingold, the name of a former Franconian-Swabian border.

Dinkelsbühl deserves special mention among the Franconian imperial cities. The city received its imperial free status neither by decree nor in return for income paid to the emperor. Nor did it become an imperial free city in order to be able to coin its own money. Instead, it was the ambition of its burghers to buy themselves free from the rights and tax privileges of the local nobility. Nevertheless, the emperor continually mortgaged the rights to the city and the burghers had to pay to redeem these mortgages time and again.

And unlike other imperial free cities, Dinkelsbühl did not make the transition to the Reformation smoothly. Controversies among the various denominations and a continual change in the religious confession of the magistrates was the rule rather than the exception.

Yet in these turbulent times during the last third of the 16th century, the Deutsches Haus, the loveliest edifice in Dinkelsbühl, was erected. Remarkable for its perfect proportions and numerous carved figures, it is considered to be the most captivating half-timbered building in southern Germany. This structure stands amidst an ensemble of Renais-

sance buildings that have been carefully restored with an eye for detail. They have taken on new functions (pub, granary, covered market) and have been fully integrated into the city thanks to the initiatives of the city's citizens.

For ten days every July, the city celebrates its Children's Festival, a moving play recalling the horrifying events of the Thirty Years' War. The story is a parable of how the pious and faithful turn fate. The play in a nutshell: The blood-

Left: The intricate high cross rib vaulting in the Gothic parish church of St. George in Dinkelsbühl.
Below: Romantic Dinkelsbühl on the Wörnitz River.
Following pages: The Hezelhof, Dinkelsbühl's most delightful courtyard, displays its artistic 17th century wooden galleries.

From Medieval to Modern

A glimpse into the past with both feet firmly planted firmly in the 21st century: Middle Franconia is where the past and present meet and a blend of the two becomes obvious. There is no pure-blooded Middle Franconian; instead, he is a healthy mixture of many cultures. The geographic location in the middle of Europe and the historically favorable trade routes across the region have left their mark in numerous ways.

thirsty Swedes seize the town, force their way inside through the Wörnitz Gate and encounter a group of children that begs for pity. The Swedish commander is moved and spares the town. The play was written by a Munich court official, Ludwig Stark, in 1897 and continues to attract thousands of people year after year.

Left: Scene from the "Kinderzeche", a children's play that retells a horrifying event during the Swedish siege of the town during the Thirty Years' War.
Below: Swedish soldiers march across the Market Square past the Grain Market Hall during a performance of the "Kinderzeche".
Right: The Deutsches Haus with its richly-carved decorative facade is one of Franconia's most fetching half-timbered buildings.
Following pages: Dinkelsbühl's west city wall and its watchtowers are fully intact.

Property claims and land ownership have always played a role and continue to do so even today. Half-timbered buildings stand alongside sandstone structures; sandstone being the natural stone of choice in this region rich in geological formations.

The choice of twinned cities and regions varies as well. For example, close political, economic and social contact is maintained with the French departement Limousin at the edge of the Massif Centrale. The diversity of Middle Franconia, including its paradoxes and contradictions, is part and parcel of a way of life that is worth taking time to get better acquainted with.